MIDDLESBROUGH
as it was

●

Norman Moorsom

Front Cover: Corporation Road, early this century.
Back Cover: Linthorpe Road, about the same period.

Published by Hendon Publishing Company Limited, Hendon Mill, Nelson, Lancashire.
Text © Norman Moorsom 1976
Printed by: Fretwell & Brian Ltd, Howden Hall, Silsden, Keighley, Yorks.

Introduction

The name "Middlesbrough" refers today to one of the four Districts which make up the County of Cleveland, inaugurated on April 1st., 1974. Exactly six years earlier to the day, the County Borough of Middlesbrough had been amalgamated with five other local Authorities to form the County Borough of Teesside. For the purposes of the present study, "Middlesbrough" refers basically to the town which became a Municipal Borough in 1853 and a County Borough in 1889.

Middlesbrough's historical reputation is that of a 19th century boom town which sprang into existence as a centre of the iron and steel industry, just as the gold-rush settlements emerged in the United States of America. There are, however, more deeply-rooted links with the past than those so generally associated with the image of the mid-Victorian Ironopolis.

In gathering together the following selection of prints and photographs of my own home town, I have attempted to turn the clock back to scenes of everyday life, and to show buildings of interest and local characters whose lives were intertwined with the growth of the town. At the same time, I hope that my readers may be led to a keener awareness of today's townscape, which is constantly changing as old properties are demolished and replaced, new roads are laid down and new estates are planned. With the aid of camera and note book, each of us can play our own part in recording for future generations the everyday scenes of the '70's.

Most of the illustrations in my book are at least 50 to 100 years old, but several of the photographs were taken within the last two decades. It is interesting to realise that if we photograph a building today and it is demolished tomorrow, we have added to the illustrative record of "Middlesbrough as it was".

Norman Moorsom
May 1976

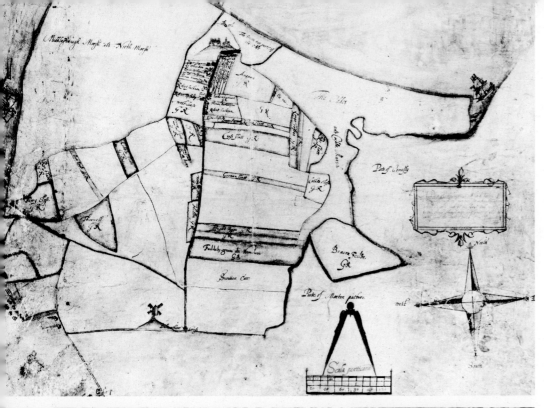

The earliest recorded settlement at Middlesbrough was a Benedictine monastic cell, which seems to have arisen as a "middle place" for monks travelling between Whitby and Durham, and it is quite possible that the place-name itself is derived from this geographical fact. The church at Middlesbrough was first mentioned in the 11th century, later became known as the Middlesbrough Priory, and was closed by 1537 during the Dissolution of the Monasteries by Henry VIII. The Priory church can be seen on "A plan of the scite, Cell and Towne of Middlesbrough", which was produced by John Gibbons in January 1618. It is believed that at this time the former church building was being used as a dwelling.

The map of 1618 shows in Middlesbrough a pattern of named strips of land and a number of houses. The main north-south axis is Linthorpe Lane, later to be known as Linthorpe Road. In the late 1950's, when work was in progress on the general re-development of the area, a number of stone-walled cellars was discovered, and it was considered at the time that they may well have been the remains of properties existing in the year 1618 which had apparently been incorporated in buildings erected when the modern town was being constructed in the 1830's.

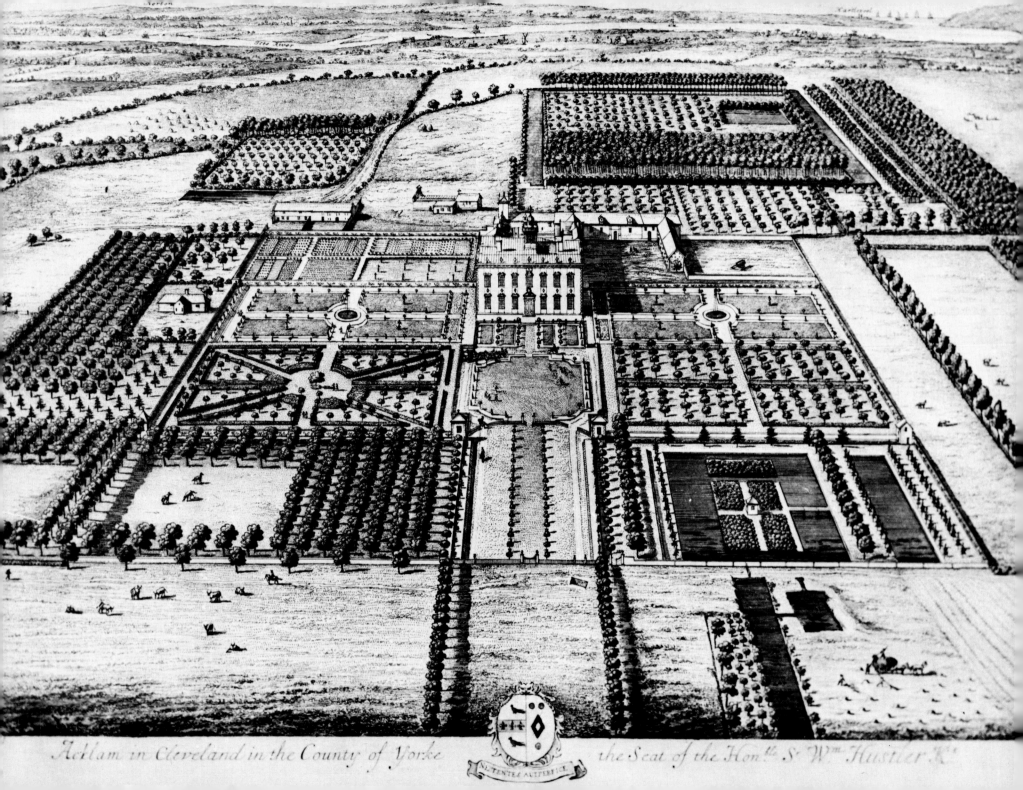

Acklam in Cleveland in the County of Yorke   *the Seat of the Hon.ble S.r W.m Hustler K.t*

Left. The monastic church at Middlesbrough is not mentioned in the Domesday Book of 1086, but reference is made to a church and a priest at Acklam, an ancient settlement which was later to be engulfed as a suburb of Middlesbrough itself. From the year 1637, the Hustlers were Lords of the Manor of Acklam, and during the reign of Charles II they built Acklam Hall. The early 18th. century engraving by Kipps shows the Hall in its original simple form, in the impressive setting of the well-planned Acklam estate. Set back north-west of the Hall is Acklam Church.

Top right. Several churches have occupied this site at Acklam, the one illustrated dating from the second half of the 18th. century. This particular building had an interesting link with a chapel which was built at Ayresome, in the township of Newport, earlier in the same century. The chapel, which was constructed from materials taken from the ruins of the Middlesbrough Priory, was never actually consecrated and gradually became a ruin itself. In about 1776, the seats and pulpit were removed to the church at Acklam, which in its turn did not have a very long life. It was demolished just prior to 1874, when Thomas Hustler had erected the original portion of the present church. The modern building is dedicated to St. Mary and was considerably enlarged in 1957 in order to cater for the needs of the population of an expanding residential area.

Bottom right. The Hustlers left the Acklam estate in the 1930's and the Hall was adapted as a Grammar School for Boys. In the photograph of 1955, it still retains its original character, but the last few years have seen the addition of new wings and the erection of new teaching blocks. The Hall itself contains a number of interesting features, including plaster ceilings bearing the date 1683.

Top left. A decade or so before the construction of Acklam Hall, the Hustlers erected a granary and a quay at Newport, which at that time was a community quite distinct from both Acklam and Middlesbrough. Here, small ships would lighten their loads into barges before continuing further up the dangerous course of the River Tees to Stockton. On their return journey, they would receive consignments of grain. The granary and adjoining Newport House was situated north of the present Ayresome Road, being demolished some 40 years ago.

Bottom left. It is generally accepted that the Middlesbrough Priory church and buildings had fallen into a state of disrepair by the second half of the 17th. century. The actual shell of the church itself was subsequently incorporated into the dwelling house of the Middlesbrough Farm. The sketch dates from the year 1808, when John and Rebecca Parrington became tenants of the owner, William Chilton of Billingham. This was to be the last tenancy, for in 1829 the farm was purchased by the business consortium which became known as the Owners of the Middlesbrough Estate, or simply the Middlesbrough Owners. It was they who were to be responsible for leading Middlesbrough into its own industrial revolution.

Facing page:
Top left. The Parringtons had a family of six sons and it is Tom, the youngest, who has come to be regarded as a particularly interesting character in the story of Middlesbrough's transition from a rural hamlet to an industrial giant. He was born in the Middlesbrough Farm House on June 20th. 1818, and at the age of 11 he saw the first brick of the first house in the modern town being laid in West Street. He and his brothers used to play on the burial ground of the Middlesbrough Priory, and he himself had his lessons at Acklam Vicarage with the Rev. Isaac Benson. In later life, Tom became renowned as an agriculturalist and a sportsman, and he died at Kirbymoorside on March 28th. 1915, at the age of 96. By this time, Middlesbrough had a population of over 100,000, whereas when Tom was born there it was only 40.

Top right. The Rev. Isaac Benson became Vicar of Acklam in the year 1823 and was also responsible for the spiritual welfare of the people of Middlesbrough, Ayresome, Linthorpe and Newport. In 1840, Middlesbrough had its own Parish Church, which was dedicated to St. Hilda of Whitby as had been the Priory church itself. Isaac Benson automatically became the first curate in charge of St. Hilda's, a position which he held until his death in 1864. When an old man himself, Tom Parrington recalled that Benson was a firm disciplinarian as an instructor, and that he had personally felt the effects of the Vicar's birch rod.

Bottom left. During the last 25 years of his life Tom Parrington was a friend of John (later Major') Fairfax Blakeborough, who recalled travelling to Middlesbrough with him in his phaeton in about 1890. Tom was to pass on to him his own love of the sporting life, together with a fund of information about his memories of Old Middlesbrough. At one time, the Major had access to Tom's journals, which were full of detail about local Hunts and the daily routine of work on the Middlesbrough Farm. I myself had the privilege of a personal interview with the Major in 1971, when he passed on to me a selection of Tom's recollections and anecdotes. He died in January 1976 at the age of 93. Between them, the Major and Tom Parrington had outlived the whole history of modern Middlesbrough, since with the inauguration of the County Borough of Teesside in 1968 the town had lost its individual identity.

Bottom right. Joseph Pease (1799–1872) was a son of Edward Pease of Darlington, one of the principal pioneers and founders of the Stockton & Darlington Railway Company, the basic aim of which was to convey coal from the pits of County Durham to the port of Stockton, on the River Tees. The Railway became operational on September 25th. 1825, and within a few months it became clear that the Tees at Stockton was too shallow for vessels of any considerable tonnage. For this reason, it was decided to erect shipping staithes at deeper water further downstream, a site at Middlesbrough on the Yorkshire bank being chosen in preference to one at Haverton Hill on the Durham bank.

The Middlesbrough Farm covered a total area of some 500 acres, its northern boundary probably being the high-water mark of the tidal mud. The present Southfield Road takes its name from its situation on the southern boundary, while the North Riding Infirmary on Newport Road stands on the western limit. To the east, the boundary followed the old course of Marton Beck. (continued next plate).

In the course of time, when roads were made to Cargo Fleet, Ormseby and Marton, tolls were collected from traffic where these roads crossed the farm boundaries. The toll bars were finally abolished in the year 1916. The photograph of the Cargo Fleet, left, and North Ormesby, below, toll bars are interesting in their portrayal of local modes of transport.

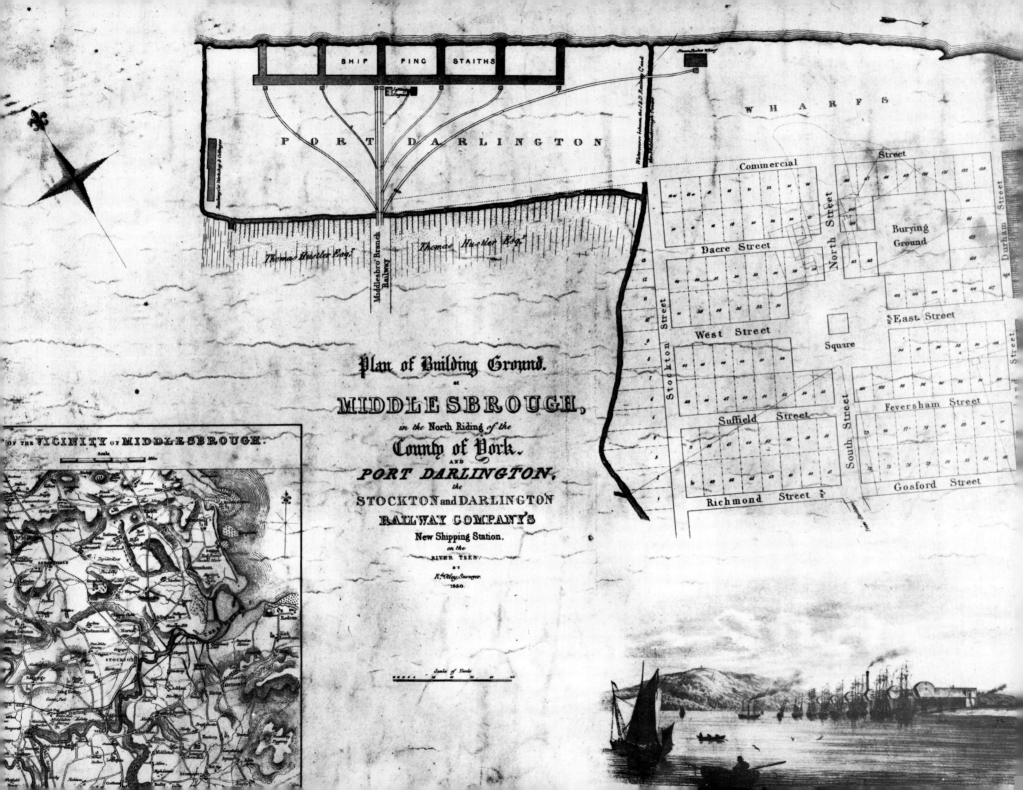

SHIP PING STAITHS

WHARFS

PORT DARLINGTON

Thomas Hustler Esq.   Thomas Hustler Esq.

Middlesbro Branch Railway

Commercial   Street

North Street

Burying Ground

Dacre Street

Durham Street

Stockton Street

West Street

Square

$ East Street

Suffield Street

South Street

Feversham Street

Richmond Street   Gosford Street

Plan of Building Ground,
at
MIDDLESBROUGH,
in the North Riding of the
County of York,
AND
PORT DARLINGTON,
the
STOCKTON and DARLINGTON
RAILWAY COMPANY'S
New Shipping Station,
on the
RIVER TEES.
BY
R. Otley, Surveyor.
1830.

Scale of Yards

OF THE VICINITY OF MIDDLESBROUGH.

Scale

Left. By 1830, the new town of Middlesbrough was being laid down, based on the survey and plan of Richard Otley of the Stockton & Darlington Railway Company. The 32-acre site was divided into a series of 123 plots, which were offered for general sale. Each plot of land measured 200 feet by 60 feet, and it was envisaged that the town would cater for a population of 5,000. However, this total was passed within the first decade and additional streets, alleys and yards were run in within the well-spaced grid of the 1830 plan.

Top right. The Stockton & Darlington Railway Company's coal-shipping staithes at Middlesbrough were 450 yards long and could accommodate six vessels for loading at one time, with berths for others in between the drops. The first coal was actually shipped here on December 27th. 1830, a date which marks the completion of the major extension of the main line of the railway system. The name originally given to the area of the shipping staithes was "Port Darlington", but this led to objections from the people of Stockton and the name was dropped.

In the foreground of this print from the early 1840's can be seen a boat operating the ferry between Middlesbrough and Port Clarence, at the point on the Tees now occupied by the Transporter Bridge.

DROPS AND SHIPPING ON THE TEES,

PREVIOUS TO THE CONSTRUCTION OF MIDDLESBOROUGH DOCKS.

Published by W. Fordyce, Newcastle.

Bottom right. "Port Clarence" was the name given to the coal-shipping facilities which were established at the termination of the Clarence Railway. This particular railway project was inspired by Christopher Tennant, and his plans matured in opposition to those in hand for the extension of the S. & D. main line from Stockton to Middlesbrough. Indeed, the Act of Parliament which authorised his scheme was passed in the same year (1828) as that for the "Quaker line" to Middlesbrough. However, it was not until the year 1833 that the first coal was shipped from Port Clarence itself, due to opposition and delays. Christopher Tennant named his railway in honour of the Duke of Clarence, who became King as William IV in 1830.

PORT CLARENCE IN 1830

SITE OF MIDDLESBROUGH, 1830.

View taken from about Lloyd & Co. Works.

Left. A coal train is here seen approaching the River Tees at Middlesbrough, being drawn by a locomotive of a type similar to the famous "Locomotion" which drew the inaugural train at the opening of the main line of railway in 1825. On the rise behind the train is the Middlesbrough Farm house, which in the sale of 1830 was purchased by Robert Manners, who used the premises as the "Middlesbrough Hotel". The range of the Cleveland Hills is seen in the distance, with Eston Nab surmounted by its original beacon, which was erected as a coastal look-out during the troubled period of the Napoleonic Wars.

Right. The proprietors of the Stockton & Darlington Railway made no provision for the erection of houses at Port Darlington, and it was entirely due to the efforts of the Middlesbrough Owners that such provision was made, and that the houses were built to an acceptable standard.

The first house in the new town was built in West Street by George Chapman in April 1830. The first tenant was Robert Morrow, who was the proprietor of the King William IV public house next door. The house itself was demolished in September 1959, and the plaque recording its unique place in Middlesbrough's history is now preserved in the town's Dorman Memorial Museum.

It is interesting to note that the son of George Chapman, John Richard Chapman, was the first child to be born in the new town of Middlesbrough. Born on August 22nd. 1830, his birth was registered at Acklam Church, since it was to be another ten years before Middlesbrough had a Parish Church of its own.

MIDDLESBROUGH IN 1832.

By permission of Sir Hugh Gilzean Reid, J.P., D.L.

Top left. The King William IV public house, commonly referred to as the "King Billy", can be seen on the general view of West Street when demolition had already started. The steepness of the main streets radiating from the Market Square is clearly seen here, underlining the fact that the town was laid out on rising ground. In ancient times, this mound would have been an island surrounded by marshes, and this fact of it being a "middle place" of dry land has been put forward as another possible origin for the place-name itself.

Bottom left. Early building progress in Middlesbrough can be seen from the sketch of 1832, reputedly drawn from a vantage point near the present St. Hilda's School in Snowden Road. The Middlesbrough Farm House and outbuildings can be seen to the left, appearing in a strange way to be aloofly surveying the infant town spreading out below. Most of the buildings on the sketch have been demolished, but the Ship Inn, clearly named on a gable end, is still standing in Stockton Street. It received its licence in 1831 and is now the oldest surviving building "over the border"—that is, north of the Darlington-Saltburn railway line.

In the early days, Middlesbrough was a boisterous place and appears to have had its own share of trouble-makers, many of whom presumably spent some time in the lock-up, which is the small building standing forward on its own in the right foreground of the sketch.

Top left. The first school in modern Middlesbrough was erected in Stockton Street in 1837. It was founded by the British and Foreign School Society on a site presented by the Middlesbrough Owners. It was to be used by the infant poor of the town, children of the labouring and manufacturing classes of any denomination, and catered for 120 boys and 100 girls. After the passing of the Education Act of 1870, Stockton Street was re-opened as one of the first Board Schools in the country. Latterly, it stood empty for some time and was finally demolished in 1960.

Bottom left. In 1858, a grammar school was opened by Dr. William Grieves on the corner of Corporation Road and Albert Road. The curriculum included an impressive selection of academic subjects, ranging from religious and moral instruction to numerous languages, history, geography, mathematics and the sciences. The school was for both boarders and day pupils, with a scale of fees which varied accordingly. It closed in 1875, when Dr. Grieves died, and the site was later acquired by the grocery firm of Amos Hinton and Sons for their Corporation Road branch. The premises are now occupied by Local Government offices and a bank.

Top left. The Middlesbrough High School was opened in January 1877 on a site at the southern end of Albert Road. The land was made available by a member of the Pease family, and this blocking-off of Albert Road made inevitable the development of Linthorpe Road as the main artery of the town. Prior to the erection of the new building, the school had occupied premises in Grange Road. The aim was to provide for the middle classes a sound education, and preparation at 13 for the Cambridge Local Examinations. In time, the 1877 premises were extended and became separate Grammar Schools for Boys and Girls. In 1959, a move was made to new buildings on the Marton Road Prissick Base and the old schools were used as a Further Education Centre. The Boys' wing (to the left of the clock tower in this photograph of about 1900) was later demolished to make way for extensions to the Teesside Polytechnic, of which complex the remainder of the old building now forms a small part.

Bottom left. In 1892, the Grange Road Schools were opened by Alderman (Sir) Hugh Bell. They offered accommodation for Senior Boys, Senior Girls, Junior Mixed and Infant pupils. Six years later, the name was changed to Hugh Bell Schools, then from 1907 it was referred to as a Higher Grade School. In 1955, the Stainsby Schools at Acklam were opened for pupils transferred from the Grange Road premises, the latter subsequently being occupied by children from a number of the old town schools. The site is now occupied by the new Law Courts, which were opened on February 2nd. 1973 by Lord Hailsham.

Top left. The first religious service in modern Middlesbrough was held in a brickyard hut in 1828. It was led by a Methodist local preacher as a means of catering for the spiritual needs of the men working on the erection of the coal-shipping staithes. The first actual place of worship in the town was built by the Methodists in West Street, close to the town's first house, in the year 1833. However, this chapel soon proved to be too small for the growing population and a new one was built in the north-west corner of the Market Place. Opened in the year 1839, it was named Centenary, as this year marked the actual centenary of the founding of Methodism by John Wesley. The cost of the building was £1,200 and it seated 500. The chapel, seen here to the right of the lamp post in the foreground, ended its days as a warehouse and the adjacent hall, which was opened in 1932, was also used for business purposes. The premises were demolished in August 1959.

Bottom left. After the disappearance of the Priory church, the people of Middlesbrough had become accustomed to relying on the church at Acklam to cater for their spiritual needs. However, by 1836 it was felt that the up-and-coming young town needed an actual Parish Church of its own. The foundation stone of St. Hilda's Church was laid in July 1838 and the building was consecrated on September 25th. 1840, with a seating capacity of 600. The site was given by the Middlesbrough Owners and the cost of the building was over £2,500, a sum which was raised through the efforts of all religious denominations in the town. The addition of a gallery in 1861 increased the seating capacity to 900, but in its closing years St. Hilda's only had a congregation of some three dozen, due to the gradual dispersal of the local population. The church fell into a state of disrepair and was finally demolished in 1969-70.

It should be pointed out that the illustration is taken from the Architect's drawing of the church, which should be compared with the actual photograph of it appearing on page 20.

Top left. St. Hilda's Church contained a full peal of eight bells, installed in 1864 through the generosity of local clergy, industrialists and citizens. These individuals and firms included Joseph Pease; H. W. F. Bolckow; John Vaughan; the Revs. Isaac Benson and Richard Bradley; Clay Lane and South Bank Iron Companies; Gilkes, Wilson Company; Cochrane and Company, and Hopkins and Company. After demolition, the bells were kept in store for a number of years, but have now been hung in a campanile behind All Saint's Church, on the corner of Linthorpe Road and Grange Road. Gone, however, are the days of the bell-ringing team, for operation is now electrical.

Cemetery, Middlesborough, Yorkshire

Bottom left. Before St. Hilda's Church was opened, use was still made of the burial ground formerly attached to the Middlesbrough Priory. On these occasions, the burials were registered at Acklam and a room in the Middlesbrough Farm house was used as a mortuary chapel. The new church had its own enclosed church-yard and the first burial there took place on October 2nd. 1840. The churchyard itself only covered a small area and was closed in August 1854.

During the following year, the question of a new burial ground became an important issue at the Vestry Meetings at St. Hilda's. A Burial Board was established, eight acres of land in Linthorpe Lane was purchased from Miss Eliza Juliana Hustler and the Middlesbrough Cemetery was laid out. After over a century of use, the cemetery was itself closed and the area is now set out as Ayresome Gardens, on the corner of Linthorpe Road and Parliament Road.

Left. In 1846, Robert Manners demolished the Middlesbrough Farm house, which he had been using as an hotel, and built the new "Middlesbrough Hotel" on the same site. During the course of the demolition, numerous relics of the ancient Priory church were brought to light, including windows, oak beams and stone fragments. Several pieces of sandstone were built into a gable of the Hotel, later moved to the main porch of St. Hilda's Church, then subsequently preserved by the Museums Service.

Left. The Middlesbrough Hotel was situated in North Street—the black-fronted building with its name printed on the gable end, standing some 40 yards north of St. Hilda's Church. It was demolished in 1963, together with all the buildings seen here in Church Place, dominated by the Transporter Bridge. This area is now occupied by one of the blocks of Council flats which are a common feature of the St. Hilda's area today.

Right. In the forecourt of St. Hilda's Church stood a monument to Robert Manners and his family, even though he himself is buried at Stainton. At one time, the monument had been allowed to fall into a state of disrepair, and renovation took place at the request of a member of the family. Unfortunately, during the demolition of the church, the monument itself was also disposed of.

The demolition of the 1960's also accounted for most of the buildings seen here on the opposite side of North Street to St. Hilda's Church. The building faced with scaffolding on the corner of Commercial Street has, however, survived to the present day. Built originally as the Middlesbrough Exchange and Hotel, later used as an annex to the old Town Hall, it has been the Custom House for some 90 years. It was here, in 1838, that His Royal Highness the Duke of Sussex, uncle of the recently-crowned Queen Victoria, was entertained to breakfast. At the time, the Duke was a guest of the Earl of Zetland and generously agreed to be the first member of the Royal Family to visit the young town.

The Tyne-Tees Wharf, across Commercial Street from the Custom House, stood on the site of the original Port Darlington. The corner wall of St. Hilda's Church, on the right in the photograph, shows how close the centre of the 1830 town was to the coal-shipping staithes which were its *raison d'etre*.

In 1841, local government in Middlesbrough had passed from the hands of the original Middlesbrough Owners into the care of a body of Improvement Commissioners, established by Act of Parliament in that year. At a meeting of the Commissioners held on March 16th. 1845, it was unanimously agreed "that it would be beneficial to the Interest of the Town that a Building should be erected in the centre of the Market Place to comprise a large room for the Town Meetings, Commissioners' room, a Market lockup & House for the Superintendant of the Police". Architects were invited to submit plans for the building and those of William Moffatt of Doncaster were accepted. The building was opened in 1846 and subsequently underwent extensions to accommodate sections of the Market itself.

Middlesbrough Market had been opened in December 1840, in its own way representing a further improvement to the amenities of the town. On the day of its opening "the scene had rather the appearance of a fair than that of a common market. Numerous banners floated in the breeze; whilst the congregated showmen trumpeted forth their monstrosities to gaping groups of wondering spectators. . ."

Top left. An overflow to the Market used to be held in South Street, seen here in 1857, but the only market now held in the immediate vicinity of Middlesbrough is at North Ormesby. The old Town Hall is seen here with its additional accommodation for the Market facing straight down South Street. Once again, there is the impression of the slope of the "compass" streets, and one finds oneself imagining the unattended barrel rolling away and causing consternation to the two housewives who are so intent on buying their fish.

Bottom left. The Old Town Hall was used as the Police Station until 1852, with cells in the basement, but after the incorporation of Middlesbrough in the following year use was made of the Exchange Hotel in North Street. Here was the lock-up and the residence of the Superintendent of Police. By 1874 the Police force consisted of a Chief Constable, two night Inspectors, two detectives, nine sergeants and 39 constables, with the services of one clerk. In 1886, the force moved into the new Town Hall in Albert Road, three years before it was officially opened. In 1902, Henry Riches became Chief Constable, and he is seen here with his senior officers in the year 1910.

Left. It would appear that Middlesbrough had a fire engine in 1855, and that this was manned by the Police. in 1871, the Fire Brigade possessed two engines and a hose roll and four years later it was decided that the rapid growth of the town warranted the provision of a central fire station. Premises were erected in Dunning Road and a new steam fire engine was presented to the Corporation by Joseph Whitewell Pease, on behalf of the Middlesbrough Owners. This engine was replaced in 1905 by an appliance named "The Erimus". Superintendent Harry Gear is seen here with this appliance and some of Middlesbrough's first regular firemen.

Top right. The foundation stone of the new Town Hall and Municipal Buildings was laid on October 24th. 1883. The architect was George Gordon Hoskins of Darlington and the total cost of the building was £130,000. It was opened by the Prince and Princess of Wales (later King Edward VII and Queen Alexandra) on January 23rd. 1889. This was the year in which Middlesbrough received the status of a County Borough.

To the south of the new building was the open space known as the "Dark Continent". It was used at one time as a cattle market and later for such functions as circuses and exhibitions. Eventually, it was decided that it should be laid out as an ornamental garden, being opened to the public as Victoria Square on July 12th. 1901.

Passing the Town Hall along Albert Road can be seen a vehicle of the Imperial Tram Company, which in 1878 took over the running of the former Middlesbrough and Stockton Tramways Company. The system was electrified in 1897 and buses were first used in the Borough in 1914.

Bottom right. In the context of the development of local transport, it is interesting to note that the first car in Middlesbrough appeared in the year 1896. It was a $1\frac{1}{2}$ horse power Benz and was owned by George Scoby-Smith. In 1904, he owned a Locomobile with the registration number DC 1.

In 1839, Joseph Pease met in Newcastle the two partners whose destiny it was to set Middlesbrough on the road to real industrial prosperity and world renown as a centre of the production of iron and steel.

Henry William Ferdinand Bolckow, far left (1806–1878) was born in Sulten, Mecklenberg, a Grand Duchy of North Germany, the son of a country gentleman. John Vaughan, left (1799–1868) was born in Worcester, the son of a Welsh ironworker. The varied patterns of their early careers brought both men to Newcastle, where they they met and became friends. Bolckow had recently retired from a business venture with a fortune of some £50,000, while Vaughan, with only a few hundred pounds to his name, cherished dreams of founding an iron works.

It was felt that Middlesbrough was an ideal place in which to establish such a business, being within reach of all the minerals necessary for the manufacture of iron. An additional incentive to settle here was the fact that Joseph Pease was prepared to offer a site for their works at a very reasonable price.

The Middlesbrough Iron Works was established in Vulcan Street, on a site on the east side of the present Transporter Bridge, and the rolling mill commenced operations on August 5th. 1841.

In the years following the opening of the works, Bolckow and Vaughan were faced with the problem of the shortage of local suplies of iron ore. However, after a detailed survey had been carried out in the Cleveland Hills, a rich outcrop of good-quality ore was discovered, in June 1850. Their problems solved, the partners were set fair for prosperity and Middlesbrough became Iron-opolis.

Right. Henry Bolckow was honoured by his fellow townspeople in 1853, when he became the first Mayor of the newly-incorporated Municipal Borough of Middlesbrough, then in 1868 he became the first Member of Parliament to represent the new Parliamentary Borough. In 1881, when Middlesbrough celebrated its golden jubilee (a year late, because of the industrial depression), a statue of Bolckow was erected behind the new Exchange, on a site at the corner of Wilson Street and Marton Road. This statue was moved to its present position in Albert Park in the year 1925.

RAILWAY STATION, MIDDLESBROUGH

Left. John Vaughan was Mayor of Middlesbrough in 1855 and a statue to his memory was erected in Exchange Place, outside the Railway Station, in 1884. The statue was moved to Victoria Square in 1914, the cab shelter from the same place going to Albert Park.

MASONIC HALL MARTON RD

THE ROYAL EXCHANGE

RAILWAY TERMINUS

Right. The present Railway Station was erected in 1877, at a cost of over £100,000, on the site of the smaller station of 1847. The sketch of 1881 shows the spacious interior, with its glazed arched roof which was 300 yards long. The latter was removed during the Second World War.

It was not long after the first shipment of coal had been made from Middlesbrough that difficulties arose because of the situation of the jetties which had been constructed in the hope of deepening the channel of the river itself. The actual effect of these jetties was to silt up the areas near the shore, thus creating shallower water at the coal-shipping staithes. For this reason, it became clear that the loading of ships in a dock would be more practicable than the existing method at the staithes. It was also felt that without a dock Middlesbrough would not be able to keep pace with the competition of other local ports. Land was obtained in 1838 and the 9–acre Middlesbrough Dock was opened on May 12th. 1842.

Left. Middlesbrough's establishments as the new termination of the Stockton & Darlington Railway took place against the background of a campaign to improve the navigation of the River Tees from there to Stockton. The channel was very tortuous and a number of shoals (Jenny Mills Island in particular) constituted a hazard to shipping. The Tees Navigation Company, established by Act of Parliament in 1808, had already improved conditions further up-river, with the opening in 1810 of the Mandale Cut. With a view to improving the trade of Stockton by further reducing its distance from the sea, the Portrack Cut was opened in February 1831, very soon after the shipment of the first coal from Middlesbrough. In 1852, the Tees Conservancy Commissioners were established by Act of Parliament and took over the duties of the Tees Navigation Company.

The year 1860 saw the establishment of Middlesbrough as a separate customs port, independent of Stockton. In the same year, there was a very severe winter and the River Tees was actually frozen over, the vessel shown here being stranded in the ice.

Right. The original port of the River Tees was at Yarm, with its ford and its ancient bridge on the road from York to Durham. The original Stockton Bridge was erected by 1771 and Yarm gradually declined as the river's principal port. In its own turn, Stockton was to be superceded by Middlesbrough, but the latter relied on its ferry as a means of crossing the river until the Transporter Bridge was opened in the year 1911. The ferry steamer "Erimus" was launched in 1888. She carried over 900 passengers and was one of the last two steamers still in use when the ferry was wound up in 1912.

Top left. The site of the Transporter Bridge is seen here in 1897, with a vessel lying at the Deepwater Wharf. The works are those of Bolckow Vaughan and the bridge was to be erected upstream from the steamer in the centre of the channel. The idea of constructing such a bridge dated back to the year 1858 and the first design for a transporter was submitted in 1875 by Charles Smith, an engineer from Hartlepool. However, it was not until 1901 that the scheme was given serious consideration.

Permission to erect the Transporter Bridge was granted by an Act of Parliament dated July 4th 1907. It was designed by the Cleveland Bridge and Engineering Company Limited and built by Sir William Arroll and Company Limited, of Glasgow. The opening ceremony, conducted by His Royal Highness Prince Arthur of Connaught, took place on October 17th. 1911. The bridge is 850 feet long, with a span of 570 feet over the water and supporting pillars 225 feet in height.

Bottom left. Communications between North Yorkshire and South Durham were further improved by the construction of the Tees Newport Bridge, close to the old Newport Station. It was built in pursuance of an Act of Parliament dated June 4th. 1930 and the site is seen here in April 1931. The contractors were Dorman, Long and Company Limited and the bridge was opened on February 28th. 1934 by the Duke and Duchess of York (later King George VI and Queen Elizabeth).

Right. Seen from the air in the 1920's, central Middlesbrough presents a rigid pattern of terraced streets, with the larger bulk of places of worship, department stores, hotels and the Town Hall and Municipal Buildings. Albert Road runs north to the railway bridge in the top corner and Corporation Road dissects the photograph horizontally, behind the clock tower of the Town Hall. The whole area on the south side of Corporation Road and the west side of Albert Road as far as Grange Road (the latter being off the photograph) is now occupied by the Cleveland Centre, a complex of shops and offices.

The building on the extreme left of the Corporation Road south frontage is the Wesley Chapel, standing on the corner of Linthorpe Road.

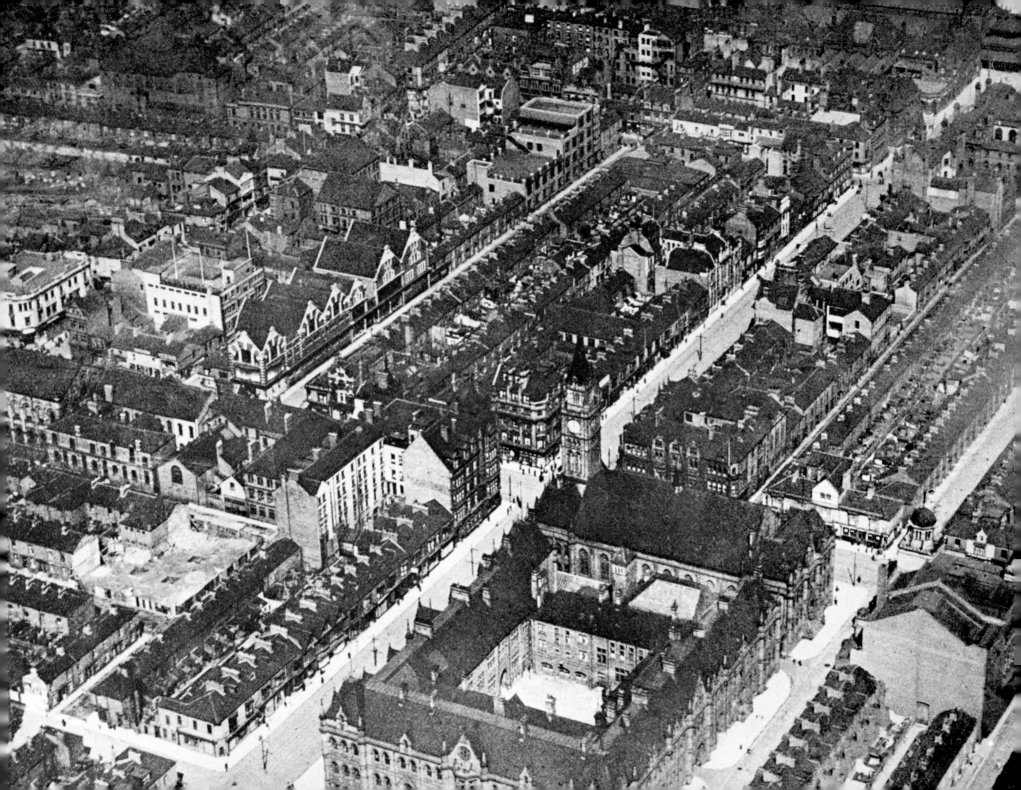

Top left. "Big Wesley", as the chapel was popularly known, was built at a cost of £6,000 and had seating for 840. It was opened on September 20th. 1863 and came to be recognised as the finest Nonconformist place of worship in the town. There was also a Day School which had a high reputation in its own right.

The congregation of the Centenary Chapel in the Market Place joined forces with Big Wesley in 1929, then in 1953 the joint congregation moved on to amalgamate with the Park Wesley Chapel. The Corporation Road site was sold to British Home Stores and Big Wesley was demolished.

Bottom left. With Big Wesley on the left, Linthorpe Road is seen here looking south. Soon after the chapel was demolished, the site of the Manfield boot store opposite was also cleared, being replaced by the multi-storey premises of Binns Ltd.

This section of Linthorpe Road itself is now closed off as a pedestrian precinct, and it is interesting to see that at the beginning of the century the absence of traffic already allowed shoppers to use it as such, with a group of men actually standing chatting in the middle of the road.

Right. As it continues its journey south, Linthorpe Road passes Southfield Road on the left, thus crossing the old boundary of the Middlesbrough Farm. The map of 1618 shows this junction and names the area on the south side as "Swatter Carr". Here stood Swatter's Carr farm house, which appears to have been demolished during the second half of the 19th. century. The site was subsequently used for fairs and amusements, the Cleveland Agricultural Society also holding its show there in the year 1879.

In the year 1900, it was decided to use the same site for the erection of an opera house. The Grand Opera House was opened on December 7th. 1903 and is seen here in 1926, under the shadow of St. George's Congregational Church. After a quarter of a century of presenting comic and grand opera, musical comedies and other entertainments, the theatre was closed. It re-opened in March 1931 as the Gaumont Cinema, having undergone a complete internal transformation. In its turn, the Gaumont itself was closed, the last film being shown in February 1964. The site has since been cleared and still awaits re-development.

THE GRAND OPERA HOUSE.

Top left. On the opposite side of Linthorpe Road to the Gaumont and south of St. George's Church, stood Victoria Buildings, headquarters of the Middlesbrough Co-operative Society. Built on the corner of Clifton Street at a cost of £16,000, the premises were opened in 1899. There were four shops on the ground floor, with other departments, offices and warehouses on the first. The second floor was taken up by the Victoria Hall, kitchens and other rooms. The building was unique in the town, with its introduction of an electrically-operated pneumatic cash carrier. In July 1942, the building was destroyed during an air raid and the Co-op has since redeveloped the site.

Bottom left. Continuing further south, Linthorpe Road led to the Middlesbrough Cemetery, which was opened in 1855. In this pre-First World War photograph which is looking north, the cemetery trees are seen on the left. The chapel in the centre is Park Wesley. The neat row of houses has been converted into a series of shops and other businesses, but the first floor windows are still recognisable. This fact is also true of many other business premises throughout the whole length of Linthorpe Road. As the town expanded, new houses were built on the southern outskirts, but continued expansion led to the need for shops and conversion became the pattern.

Top left. St. Aidan's Lodge was one of the elegant villas on Linthorpe Road, standing on the opposite side to the Park Wesley Chapel. In 1890, the citizens of Middlesbrough are seen taking the air, while a cab makes its leisurely way along what is now a very busy bus route. St. Aidan's Lodge was the residence of G. H. S. Godwin, a cousin of Lord Tennyson, and reputedly descended from Godwin, King of the Saxons. The site is now occupied by students' halls of residence.

Diagonally opposite Park Wesley is the entrance to Albert Park itself. Covering an area of over 70 acres, the Park was presented to the townspeople of Middlesbrough by Henry Bolckow, at a personal cost of £30,000. It was opened on August 11th. 1868 by Prince Arthur (later Duke) of Connaught and named after the late husband of Queen Victoria.

Bottom left. The Park originally had three lakes, the upper one being known as the Cannon Lake. In 1857, Lord Panmure had presented to the town a cannon from the Battle of Sebastopol in the Crimean War and it was eventually placed by the Park lake. It remained there until 1949, when two of the lakes were filled in. The cannon now stands in front of the Territorial Army premises on Stockton Road. Another interesting relic at this lake was an archway said to have been constructed from a window of the ancient Middlesbrough Priory church. Seen here in 1908, the archway was later demolished and a number of stones preserved for local interest.

Top left. Linthorpe Road originally led to the village of that name, a separate community which in the course of time became a suburb of the expanding Middlesbrough. On the corner of the present Burlam Road and Roman Road stood the Blue Hall, reputedly used by smugglers from Newport. The Hall was demolished in 1870 and the site is now occupied by a bakery. The Middlesbrough map of 1618 shows several houses at "Linthrop", in the lower left corner, and the Blue Hall may well be the building shown just above the village name itself.

Bottom left. Several of the white cottages from Old Linthorpe survived in St. Barnabas' Road, where they stood out into the roadway from the building line of the modern houses. Seen here looking towards Linthorpe Road, the cottages were demolished in May 1935.

Right. The Linthorpe Pottery was established in the year 1879 by John Harrison, on the site of his Sun Brick Works. He was aided by Dr. Christopher Dresser, a celebrated architect and designer, who first noted the suitability of the local clay for the manufacture of high class products. The speciality of Linthorpe ware was in its glaze and the boldness of its colours, many pieces now being preserved in the Dorman Memorial Museum. The Pottery proved to be an artistic success, but it was also a financial failure and ceased production in 1889. Here we see the ladies at work in the print room of the Pottery, the site of which is now occupied by a laundry.

Left. Constant reference has been made to the fact that many local buildings of interest have been demolished during the systematic re-development of Old Middlesbrough. Actual slum clearance in the St. Hilda's area began just before the outbreak of the First World War, when attention was directed towards some of the worst properties which had sprung up in between the well-spaced streets of Richard Otley's planned town. The living conditions of the local residents are shown in a series of photographs which resulted from a survey carried out in the year 1910. Take a close look at this group in Back Graham Street and let the residents span the years with their care-worn faces.

Right. The same hardened expression is seen here on the faces of the St. Hilda's people as they queue for water. This would be a routine aspect of life in the "yards", where there was a communal tap to be shared by a number of households. Here are the women with their buckets and jugs, their numerous children and the odd cloth cap. Behind the window, frozen in time, are the faces of more inquisitive urchins, obviously wondering what the strange man is doing with the funny box on long legs.

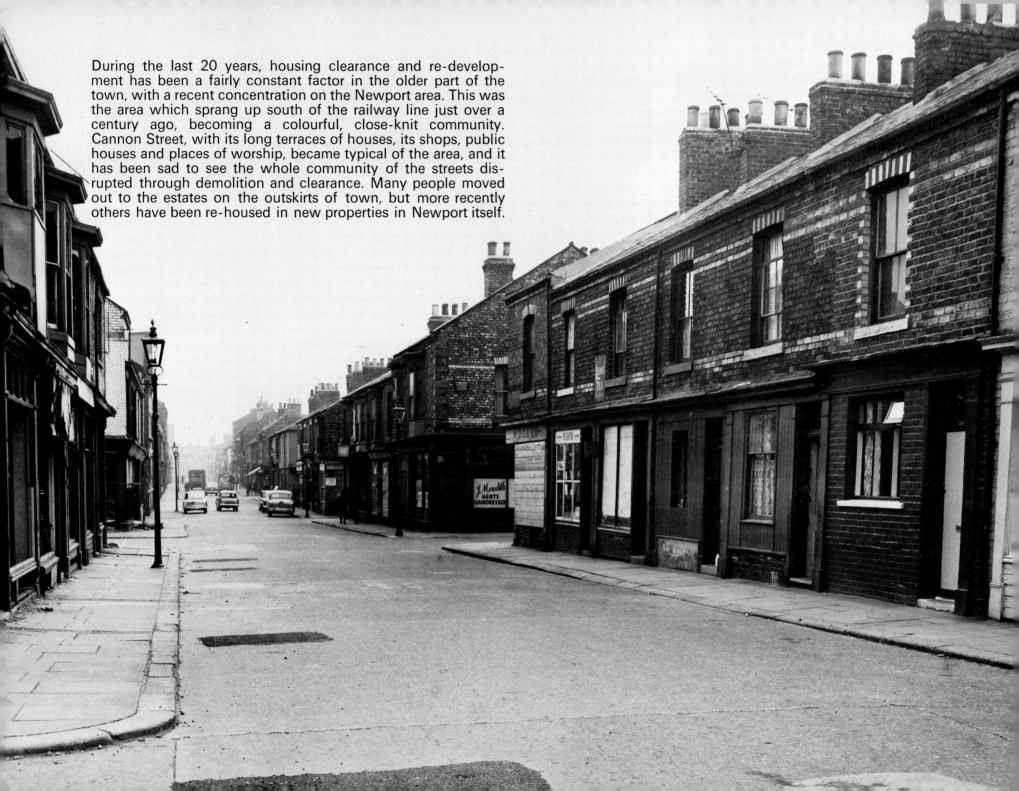

During the last 20 years, housing clearance and re-development has been a fairly constant factor in the older part of the town, with a recent concentration on the Newport area. This was the area which sprang up south of the railway line just over a century ago, becoming a colourful, close-knit community. Cannon Street, with its long terraces of houses, its shops, public houses and places of worship, became typical of the area, and it has been sad to see the whole community of the streets disrupted through demolition and clearance. Many people moved out to the estates on the outskirts of town, but more recently others have been re-housed in new properties in Newport itself.

In the private sector of housing development, there has been extensive activity in recent years on the southern fringes of Middlesbrough, and it is interesting to see how this fact has led to History repeating itself. Just as the Middlesbrough Farm buildings were cleared in 1846, so Newham Bridge Farm disappeared in 1964. The farm was situated in an area in which land was held by the Middlesbrough Priory, but the actual date of its origin is not known. It stood at the junction of Tollesby Road and Hall Drive, and its fields are now covered by the Acklam Hall Estate.

In the first Census of 1801, the population of the Township of Middlesbrough was 25, every one of whom was "chiefly employed in agriculture". The mid-1974 estimate of population for the Borough of Middlesbrough was 153,900. Very few farms are now worked in the Middlesbrough of today and they are a vanishing reminder of Middlesbrough as it was.

Norman Moorsom was born in Middlesbrough in October 1940, and was educated at Middlesbrough Boys' High School and at St. John's College of Education, York.

After teaching for ten years in Secondary Schools in and around Middlesbrough, he now works as a teacher with the position of Museum Schools Service Officer for the County of Cleveland—an area ranging from Hartlepool in the north to Loftus in the south.

He has a profound interest in the history of Middlesbrough and district and has written over a dozen books on the subject.

As a consequence of spending so much time in Middlesbrough Reference Library during programmes of research, he met and married the Senior Assistant Reference Librarian and has a son, Richard, and a daughter, Hilary.

If you have enjoyed this book—one of many in the *As It Was* series—why not send for our list of existing and intended titles?

Acknowledgements: The author wishes to thank all who helped make this book possible. Most of the illustrations were made available by the County of Cleveland Libraries Department and the County Planning Department. The copyright of others is vested in the Public Record Office, Dennis Wompra, and Cleveland Constabulary.

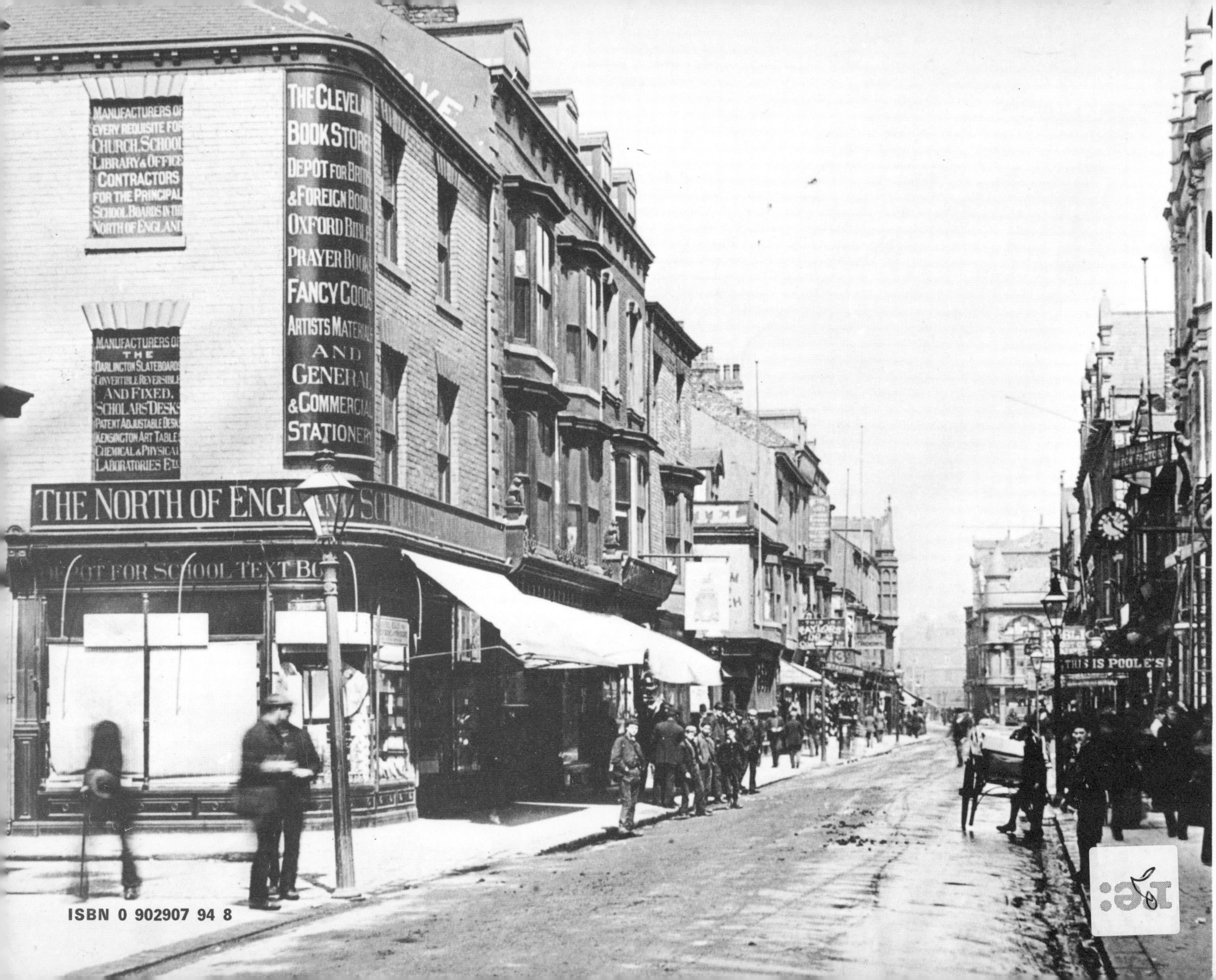

ISBN 0 902907 94 8

MIDDLESBROUGH AS IT WAS

Moorsom

COALS FROM NEWCASTLE

An Introduction to the Northumberland and Durham Coalfield
by Les Turnbull